TTI SUCCESS INSIGHTS®

TALENT / UNKNOWN

7 WAYS TO DISCOVER HIDDEN TALENT + SKILLS

BY BILL J. BONNSTETTER & ASHLEY BOWERS

ISBN 978-0-9707531-8-2

THANKS TO EMILY SOCCORSY,
FOR HER EDITORIAL SUPPORT
AND ASSISTANCE.

7 WAYS TO
DISCOVER
YOUR HIDDEN
TALENT + SKILLS

CONTENTS

INTRODUCTION

It is not unusual to see the word "talent" used interchangeably with the word "skill." **In fact, the two are quite different entities, two halves of a whole of human potential.** For the purposes of this guide, skills are a person's developed aptitude, the learned ability to use one's knowledge effectively. Talent is the convergence of a person's skills and abilities, knowledge and experience matched with his or her innate aptitude.

Talent is the convergence of a person's skills and abilities, knowledge and experience matched with his or her innate aptitude.

Talent encompasses many different dimensions of human behavior. Each is equally important in the process of uncovering a person's own potential. **If we were more aware of what our own talents and skills were, how much more could we accomplish?**

Imagine if each of us was born with a conscious awareness of our unique talents. Imagine we were immediately aware of the tasks we could tackle easily, the challenges we could mindlessly navigate because of our talent. What if we knew as we came of age all the skills we were likely to develop, because of our talents and our life's experience? What if we understood how we could leverage those skills to achieve our goals? The world would be limitless.

It occurs to you:
You could be sitting on an intellectual goldmine.

Imagine again you are the owner or manager of a medium or large company with dozens of employees who tend to be guarded and task-oriented around you. After all, you're the boss and they want to give the impression they are doing their job. Yet from time to time you overhear snippets of conversation that lead you to believe some of your employees have talents in unexpected areas. You begin to wonder: like an undiscovered cache of gold, how many of these talents remain hidden under the surface undetected? **Do these employees understand the depth of their hidden potential?** How valuable to your company's bottom line would those uncovered talents become once revealed, understood and applied? It occurs to you: You could be sitting on an intellectual goldmine.

Unfortunately, in business, this scenario happens far too frequently. Years ago, Bill was approached by a team of bright engineers and managers from Motorola. The team leaders had begun to think about the trove of hidden talent surrounding them.

"We don't even know what talent we have," they confided. "We believe in some cases we have people working in the wrong department." The team was well-intentioned and sincere. They asked Bill to create a system that would identify these hidden talents and a method for bringing these talents to bear for the benefit of the company. Bill gladly took on the challenge. Sadly, soon after the initial meeting, the project was cancelled due to a widespread layoff. Standing on the ledge of a hidden talent roadmap, the potential of the project persisted in Bill's memory.

Years later, Bill was visiting the office of an agricultural supplier when the managers began chatting about how pleased they were to be rid of an employee they had recently let go. With little regard for that employee's ability, competency and talents, the managers were happy to be free of this drain on resources. Several days later, during a visit Bill made to an office supply company across town, managers there were extolling the virtues of a recent hire. Bill was surprised to discover it was the person fired from the last agricultural supplier. While it might have been a case of a mismatch for one company's culture over another, we've come to believe it's also likely it was a case of undiscovered talent—talent the second company was able to identify and scoop up.

We often see the same thing in sports. Under one coach, a talented, motivated athlete does not excel and the team has a losing record. But when traded to a new team and paired with a new coach, that same talented athlete suddenly improves greatly. In this scenario, it's often the coach who recognizes talent and finds a way or a coaching system for players to make the most of both their talents and their skills.

Unfortunately, learning, identifying and discovering the talents, skills, behaviors and motivators we—or our employees—excel at is a process of trial and error, exposure and rejection. It is often difficult, sometimes painful, and can also be gloriously fun. But is there a better, more efficient way? **Can a deeper understanding of behaviors, motivators, skills and emotional intelligence help us uncover these talents in each area?** We think so.

The intent of this book is to help people discover their talents and to help employers apply these talents, thus leading to superior performance. **This book will provide a roadmap to discovering talents from seven different dimensions:**

- *Experience*

- *Education*

- *Behavior*

- *Motivators*

- *Personal Skills*

- *Acumen*

- *Emotional Intelligence*

We acknowledge Intelligence as a Dimension of Superior Performance; however, as you discover, build and learn to articulate your talents, intelligence is not a dimension we will be exploring in "Talent Unknown."

The knowledge we share in these pages is a result of years of pioneering research into individual talents, abilities, biases and experiences and how they shape each of us. We share trends, findings and reports based on this research. All we ask from our readers is an open mind. **We'll do the rest.**

WHAT TTI MEASURES

- *Behavior*
- *Acumen*
- *Personal Skills (Competencies)*
- *Motivators*
- *Emotional Intelligence*

WHAT TTI ACKNOWLEDGES

- *Experiences*
- *Education & Training*
- *Intelligence*

TTI'S DIMENSIONS OF SUPERIOR PERFORMANCE

©2013 Target Training International, Ltd.

☆TTI MEASURES

△TTI ACKNOWLEDGES

1

EXPERIENCE
Measuring Its Meaning

Alex walks into a job interview with an updated resume and hopes this interview for a drafting position with an architecture firm will lead to a good job. *The interview seems to be going well, with the employer, Ms. Smith, asking Alex about his experience. When Alex hears Ms. Smith ask, "I see you have ten years of experience in drafting. Great! Can you tell me what skills you have developed while doing that job?" his heart drops. He has no idea how to answer. Later, Alex starts to think the question itself was quite unfair.*

Brenda is up for a promotion.

She's put together a proposal for how much of a raise she believes she deserves and has a list of all the ways she has positively impacted the success of her company. When she walks into her manager's office to present her case, he throws her a curveball. He asks her, "I'm curious about how much you've grown in the five years you've been with us, Brenda. What skills have you developed during your time here?" Brenda's mind goes blank. This is not what she was expecting.

Skills built by experience accumulate slowly over time and are difficult for individuals to identify.

Translating experience into skills—whether in a job interview, performance review or while reviewing or writing a resume—is tricky business. In general, hiring managers and employers have failed to define what specific skills "X-amount" of experience delivers, yet they recognize talents, skills and experience are of critical importance. In the same way, employees with experience have not analyzed their experience to determine what skills they have really developed. The same is true of job seekers. What would be helpful to all involved is developing a process to assist people in identifying natural talents and acquired skills they have built over the years. We no longer can assume five years of experience is five years of valued experience for all people. **We believe a better way to hire would be creating a process to identify the skills and talents required by the job and then seeking an experienced person who has acquired and developed those skills.** However, most organizations do not have such a process. Therefore, it's up to each individual to be able to identify and articulate his or her own skills and talents. Skills built by experience accumulate slowly over time and are difficult for individuals to identify.

It can be even more difficult, as our examples illustrate, to say specifically how those skills were acquired. In addition, individuals might not even be aware of their natural talents, regardless of what experiences they have had.

Jobs most certainly help grow talent and build skills. Consider your most recent position and the amount of time you have held that position. Now in your mind try to list the individual skills you use on a regular basis to be successful in this position. How many can you think of?

On the following pages we've provided a few examples to help you along...

JOB: Salesperson

EXPERIENCE: Five years

SKILLS:

- *Persuasion*

- *Personal Accountability*

- *Goal Orientation*

- *Presenting*

- *Self-Management*

- *Territory Management*

- *Customer Relations*

- *Diplomacy and Tact*

- *Empathy*

- *Flexibility*

- *Competitiveness*

- *Sense of Urgency*

As you can see we have listed quite a few skills that a person may possess as a result of five years of selling experience.

JOB: Bank Teller

EXPERIENCE: Five years

SKILLS:

- *Attention to Detail*

- *Accuracy*

- *Diplomacy and Tact*

- *Customer Service*

- *Cross Selling*

- *Continuous Learning*

- *Latest Technology Skills*

- *Team Building*

- *Empathy*

- *Compliance with Regulations*

JOB: Marketing & Web Designer

EXPERIENCE: Five years

SKILLS:

- *Search Engine Optimization*

- *Business Acumen*

- *Aesthetics*

- *Creativity/Innovation*

- *Company Branding*

- *Continuous Learning*

- *Current Social Media*

- *Understanding Web Analytics*

- *Understanding Customers*

Of course, it is impossible for us to identify whether these individuals had the inherent talent for these jobs, built these skills prior to these positions or if they developed them during the five-year period. But what matters more than when the skill was acquired is identifying and articulating the skills currently in their repertoire. **When people identify and share their skills, whether they are inborn or developed, they actually use those skills more, thus refining and improving them as a part of the self-discovery process.**

These three jobs give you an idea of how you need to look at yourself and identify your real talents. The jobs listed are intended to give you only some ideas, and no way do we think we've identified all the talents a person could have acquired doing these jobs. Many jobs require continuous improvement, which may mean developing new skills and calling out different talents. Some jobs change along the way, so that an individual may no longer use old skills or talents for the job.

Possessing skills not required by your current position could be detrimental to your own performance, as well as to the performance of those around you.

Mastering a skill not needed by your job could be **detrimental to your future career.**

For example, a Winnebago facility in Forest City, Iowa, had one large room that housed about 40 engineers. One of these engineers had mastered the art of persuasion and spent a lot of time on the phone talking to people. Persuasion was not a skill required by his job and, thus, detracted from his performance and annoyed all the engineers trying to work. Mastering a skill not needed by your job could be detrimental to your future career. If this master persuader realized he was quite skilled at persuasion, he might have considered changing careers to play to his strengths.

Alternately, acknowledging and owning this talent could reduce the negative impact on his current career. He could approach his employer or supervisor and discuss this skill and ask how he could better put it to use for the company. This would also show his initiative and openness to change and new challenges. **Remember, having skills is important, but knowing what skills you have is paramount and can help pave your career path for the future.**

2

EDUCATION
An End-All-Be-All?

Do skills come from education? Some would argue they do. Yet, if that were true, each and every person who is well educated could be a smashing success. So how do we use one's education to assess his/her talents and skills?

Regardless of where or how a person is educated, the skills that are built will vary. Because education might be the most obvious detail on a resume, we may false-ly assign a higher value than it deserves. Many people are biased solely based on the university you attended, which may or may not be a true reflection of the education of any specific individual. **While education is important, it in and of itself does not tell the complete story of a person's intellect or his or her skills.**

Think of an individual's talents as a bag of coffee, chock-full of a variety of bean types, harvested from a range of groves (colleges or universities), roasted at varying temperatures (various degree programs, study skills, internships or specializations), using various roasting techniques (teaching standards, quality of faculty, family support, finances). While at a glance the beans appear alike sitting in the bag, once ground together and then brewed, a unique blend is created. Education is a part of the mix, an important one, but just a part.

But hiring an excellent student from one of the nation's most prestigious schools guarantees success, right? Not so. A 2008 study from the University of Nebraska and University of Northern Iowa investigated the grade point averages of engineering students and business majors. The results showed a strong correlation between study habit skills and success in grade point, and not just grade point average alone. Furthermore, according to research by a Target Training International study of 176 nominated entrepreneurs, there is no correlation between grade point average and serial entrepreneurship.

But hiring an excellent student from one of the nation's most prestigious schools guarantees success, right? Not so.

A focus on style type might be better placed. For instance, on the DISC (Dominance, Influence, Steadiness, Compliance) scale, individuals with a high C style tended to have higher grade point averages than the other styles. Similarly, education does not automatically provide an understanding of oneself deep enough to self-distinguish key skills.

How many people can **truly** pinpoint the skills they are proficient at and are prepared to apply to the work world?

Think of yourself when you graduated from high school or college. Most likely you were all too familiar with the question, "So, what are you going to do now?" or "What are you planning to do with your life?" For many, answers to such open questions at an ambiguous time of life proved too difficult to answer. Once the time comes to describe high school or college experience on a resume or job application the inevitable question arises: **"What did I actually learn in college?"**

How many people can truly pinpoint the skills they are proficient at and are prepared to apply to the work world? For those who found immense pleasure in the learning environment provided by formal education, it's possible they have gained the skill of continuous learning. Those who excel at continuous learning are identified in a number of ways. Students who relished the experience of going to college, attending lectures, researching, and taking a variety of courses, are proficient at continuous learning. Those who stumble into bookstores and spend hours browsing have mastered the skill of continuous learning.

So how does continuous learning apply as a skill? Jobs requiring constant education, refinement of knowledge and frequent updates require an individual with continuous learning skills. An ideal job match would require acquiring new knowledge and applying it on a regular basis. In today's technology-driven, rapidly changing work environment, education and continuous learning are key components needed in businesses running the gamut.

In addition, being skilled at continuous learning also indicates a desire to move ahead in one's career.

According to a 2011 study by Rutgers University's John J. Heldrich Center for Workforce Development, 62 percent of all recent college graduates surveyed believe they will need more formal education if they are to be successful in their chosen career. Only one in five said they believe they can have a successful career with the four-year degree they already have.

Education in and of itself does not equate to success. If all education led to success, then all educated people would be successful. Hiring managers trying to set the hiring bar high might say they are only looking to hire graduates of an Ivy League school. But not all graduates of Ivy League schools are successful, nor are they necessarily the brightest individuals in the hiring pool. Looking instead at self-awareness of one's talents or searching for the skill of continuous learning might be a more effective way of identifying top performers.

Education is a part of a person's talents but **does not reveal all** *of a person's talents and abilities.*

If education and knowledge always led to success, then all CPAs, lawyers, doctors, nurses and others who have passed a certification exam would be successful. We all know that is not true. Education is a part of a person's talents but does not reveal all of a person's talents and abilities. What do you want to continue learning about? What skills are you certain you've acquired during your education?

3

BEHAVIOR
Do You Do What You Think You Do?

Forget the fancy definitions:
Behavior is basically how you do what you do.

Forget the fancy definitions: Behavior is basically how you do what you do. So much of life and business revolves around the different ways we as human beings with unique life circumstances and approaches, behave. The importance of behavior cannot be underestimated. In fact, we've built careers on understanding and explaining the dimensions of behavior and how that impacts individuals and organizations. But how familiar are you with your own behavior? **Do you really understand how you behave and how your talents and skills are being conveyed through your behavior, as well as what key behaviors will help get you further?** How do other people's behaviors affect you? Finally, how adept are you at blending behaviors in the workplace and at home? This chapter will explore these three key facets of behavior. But first, we must examine a common list of behaviors often found in work environments.

THE FOLLOWING IS A LIST OF KEY BEHAVIORS WE HAVE MEASURED AND VALIDATED:

- *Frequent Interaction with Others*

- *Versatility*

- *Frequent Change*

- *Urgency*

- *People Oriented*

- *Competitiveness*

- *Customer Relations*

- *Follow Up and Follow Through*

- *Consistency*

- *Following Policy*

- *Analysis of Data*

- *Organized Workplace*

There are also **three key aspects of behavior** that act as integral parts of what we do and why. We'll discuss each in this chapter.

IDENTIFYING & OWNING YOUR BEHAVIORAL SKILLS

The first and most imperative part of working with people seeking help or direction in their careers is to help them identify their own behavioral style. Many tools exist to help people do this (of course, we recommend TTI's suite of assessments as the most accurate and validated on the market today). But more important than the tool you use, is how the individual digests the information. **One must truly identify with and internalize behavior in order to move on to any of the other behavioral considerations.**

Behavioral skills are important to identify and understand because it is best NOT to work in an occupation that demands behavioral skills you do not possess. When we are forced to use skills we do not possess, we become stressed. It doesn't mean we cannot accomplish what we need to, but it does mean a lot more energy and concentration will be used to accomplish the tasks which lead to stress.

Sandra is in a job that requires adherence to rules and regulations to the point of perfection.

Success in this job depends on Sandra's ability to adhere to these rules. While she loves the company she works for, she is a creative and futuristic thinker who prefers thinking outside-the-box. After taking a behavioral assessment, Sandra realizes her natural talents and behavior do not match her job. That explains why she's been feeling unmotivated and stifled by work.

Eric is a truck driver. *For Eric, the appeal of the job was in the constant movement. Eric possesses a great sense of urgency to get things done. He loves arriving at his destination and delivering his cargo on time. Unfortunately, he's also set records for the most speeding tickets and fines for overweight cargo the company has ever had. Eventually, the company becomes tired of paying for Eric's urgency-induced mistakes and they let him go.*

So, discovering your behavioral talents and finding **the appropriate career that will utilize them** *can lead to a long, healthy and happy life.*

When an individual understands behavior, he or she may then find a career that matches that talent. Certain adaptations are expected, particularly when a company or department is going through change. But, when one has to repeatedly adapt behavior for a specific job, it takes energy, which is a big cost on a person's productivity and personal health. So, discovering your behavioral talents and finding the appropriate career that will utilize them can lead to a long, healthy and happy life.

APPRECIATING OTHERS' BEHAVIOR

Once a person can own one's behavior, the next goal is to identify, understand and appreciate people who behave differently. Of those three directives, the most important is the latter—genuine appreciation of one's differences. This approach is vital in every aspect of life, and particularly in business. As a manager, an attitude of appreciation can inherently enhance the value of your team by enabling the free flow of ideas. When you can appreciate a team member for bringing in a novel idea, something totally different than you carry in to the boardroom, the result is not an affront or a fracture in the ranks. Rather, you get two great ideas.

It's easy for us to identify people who are unique. Unfortunately, all too often we see people pointing out unique individuals in a mocking way, laughing and making fun of their differences. In essence, by doing so we are alienating those who are different, instead of embracing them. We need to move past this as a society. **The more we can appreciate diversity—from childhood to the peak of our careers—the more opportunities for growth and prosperity will flourish.** It's appreciation, embodied by a positive attitude toward the other, which we need. **We need to love our differences.** That positive attitude, or affect, changes the chemistry within our bodies and opens up doors of possibility. In fact, multiple studies by Dr. Barbara L. Fredrickson, author of the book "Positivity," have shown a positive attitude can alter mindsets, widen attention spans and increase intuition and creativity.

BLENDING BEHAVIORS

After appreciating other people's behavior and ideas, we can learn how to flex and blend behavioral approaches for the benefit of all. Communication is vital to this process. Imagine a job candidate or an employee up for a promotion walking into your office and stating, "My strength is that I am very competitive." While an initial reaction might be to be threatened by that statement, what if you were able to appreciate this competitive spirit and brainstorm on how it could be marshaled for more sales for your company? Similarly, instead of being frustrated with a colleague who spends two hours reading through the new printer manual, imagine being inspired by her ability to provide stability and basic useful, knowledge essential to the function of your team. Moreover, guess who is able to fix the printer in a matter of seconds in time to print a key contract or report? Instead of grumbling over the employee who talks to everyone else too much, what about sending him out to your next conference or expo and assigning him to represent the company at its booth?

COMMUNICATION

IS VITAL TO

BLENDING BEHAVIORS

Learning about the uniqueness of your team can only help you place people where their particular talent can shine. Forget old stigmas or your own biases as to what talents are most valuable. Embrace instead the idea each person has a talent waiting to be put into play for the benefit of the organization. Be flexible about it, too. When the Apollo 11 crew made its way to the moon in 1969, they were off course for much of the journey.

Since every point of reference on the journey—the Earth, the moon, the spacecraft—were in motion during the trip, NASA was aware course corrections would be a vital part of the mission. But the crew did not make course corrections each minute of the flight. Instead, anticipating the need for constant change and course flexibility, once an hour the capsule made precise corrections. As we all know, despite spending their flight off-course, they arrived at their destination: Tranquility.

Learning about the **uniqueness** *of your team can only* **help** *you place people where their particular talent can* **shine.**

We should act in much the same way. Know your goals for your company and your team but allow for some diversity of behavior and approach on the road there. Expect detours and deviations and remain open to the behavior of each individual. As the leader, expect to step in occasionally to re-orient momentum toward your goal but do not anticipate a direct route.

Executives, business owners and hiring managers frequently tell us they cannot find the talent they are looking for. Unfortunately, our years of experience and research has told a different story, regardless of the economic climate. Employers cannot identify the talent in people when they see it. **This is mainly because people who come into an organization do not truly understand their own talent, and the organizations are not, generally, screening for them.** In some cases, businesses cannot even fathom the potential that comes along with those collective talents.

It all begins with **identifying** *behavior,* **appreciating** *behavior and then* **blending** *that behavior, based on talent, instead of on experience or education.*

Imagine a 1000-person organization as a kettle with 1000 kernels of corn in the bottom covered with oil. Once you turn on the heat, the kernels begin to pop. That is the management-driven process of uncovering talents. When the popcorn pops, it will go in all different directions. But what if you could train the popcorn to pop all at the same time and in the same direction? It could literally blow the lid off of the kettle. This explosion of talent would impact the bottom line of that organization in a tremendously significant manner.

It all begins with identifying behavior, appreciating behavior and then blending that behavior, based on talent, instead of on experience or education.

4

MOTIVATORS
Private Purposes
that Drive You

When someone discovers his or her purpose or passion in life, that person is typically energized to accomplish most of the tasks relating to that purpose.

In other words, you cannot achieve anything in life without doing something. Motivators drive us to achieve something. This motivation begins in the mind, with an idea. Once the idea has taken root, you get out of bed and start doing what it takes to bring that idea to fruition.

Motivators are very deeply held and not obviously apparent, even in the closest of relationships. It is possible to live with someone and not truly understand what motivates him. It is also possible to not really understand what motivates you. In rough times, motivators can diverge and become obscured. In a relationship, only a deep personal examination and in-depth discussion can allow motivators to be revealed. In the work environment, motivators are important to job satisfaction and performance. Once made more apparent, with the correct assessment tools, motivators provide valuable insight into ourselves and our success.

MOTIVATORS IN PRACTICE

Kristen is passionate about being outdoors and loves photography. She's built up her skills with her camera slowly over the years. The better she got at taking photographs, the more she wanted to learn about photography. She set aside money for nearly a year and eventually purchased a semi-professional camera and lighting equipment. The day she got her camera her heart was pumping with joy and anticipation. The camera augmented her repertoire of photography skills she had acquired over the years and her talent blossomed. Kristen can now capture highly artistic and poignant images that inspire others and provide a deep sense of satisfaction.

In most cases, **once we have fulfilled some of our passions, they no longer motivate us,** *so we tend to develop new passions that energize new motivations.*

Many people with passion acquire knowledge and skills as they relate to that specific passion, without even noticing they are doing so. For Kristen, eventually her talents elevated beyond just the technical skills associated with a camera and evolved into making a picture rather than just taking a picture.

In most cases, once we have fulfilled some of our passions, they no longer motivate us, so we tend to develop new passions that energize new motivations. The new motivators send us off into new directions in life. **We are also capable of having more than one set of motivators.** The more we understand our motivators, the better we are able to understand how we evolve. Before we can address the talents associated with a person's motivators, we need to help you discover your purpose and direction in life, or your own unique motivators at this moment in time.

TYPES OF MOTIVATORS

Let's look at some of the categories that identify people's passions as well as the potential skills and talents for each of the six motivators.

THEORETICAL

If you have a passion for knowledge you will enjoy many of the following:

- *Reading books*

- *Attending seminars*

- *Getting into deep discussions*

- *Going to bookstores or libraries*

- *Never quitting college*

Be aware you are likely to enjoy continuous learning, also known as continuous improvement. These are people driven by a **Theoretical Motivator.** They tend to want to gain all of the knowledge and information to be successful in a specific area. Many times this drive is so broad these individuals become experts in multiple areas. This is referred to as a "super generalist."

People with a **Theoretical Motivator** may possess the following talents and/or skills:

- *Analysis of data*

- *Writing research papers*

- *Analytical problem solving*

- *Good study habits*

- *Known as a source for knowledge and wisdom*

UTILITARIAN

If you have a passion for the future you may enjoy many of the following:

- *Creatively applying resources to solve a problem*

- *Rejecting that which you consider a waste of resources or time*

- *Futuristic thinking*

- *Working long hard hours to gain financial security*

- *Enjoying capitalistic endeavors*

You are likely to enjoy the practical pursuits and be driven by a **Utilitarian Motivator.** These people tend to want to make deals based on investment and return, to advance quickly in their chosen career and be competitively paid. Utilitarians are always expecting something in return for services rendered or time given.

People with a **Utilitarian Motivator** may possess the following talents and/or skills:

- *Futuristic thinking*

- *Problem solving*

- *Saving money/investing*

- *Solving problems with the bottom-line in mind*

- *Organizing for utility*

- *Entrepreneurial mindset*

- *Solving problems that others have failed at*

- *New product and service ideas*

AESTHETIC

If you have a passion for beauty you may enjoy many of the following:

- *The finer things in life*

- *Colors, arrangements or design*

- *Harmony and unity within your physical and relational world*

- *Being empathetic to the feelings of others*

- *Working for less money as long as the surroundings are aesthetically pleasing*

Be aware you are likely to appreciate art in all aspects of life and be driven by an **Aesthetic Motivator.** Those motivated by aesthetics have a complete life mindset. With a strong Aesthetic Motivator, you are immersed in your surroundings, actively interacting with your environment to become all you can be, with an intense passion for self-development.

People with an **Aesthetic Motivator** may possess the following talents and/or skills:

- *Creativity*

- *An aptitude for beauty, form, and harmony*

- *Efficient use of natural resources*

- *Layout and design*

- *Artistic abilities/appreciation*

- *Branding/packaging*

- *Awareness of fashion, dressing in good taste for success.*

- *Open to self-improvement*

SOCIAL

If you have a passion for others you may enjoy many of the following:

- *Investing your time, talents and resources, even without return*

- *Supporting charitable causes*

- *Giving to others, even to your own detriment*

- *Promoting fairness to people in all areas of life*

- *Preserving the classics in music, art and literature*

You are most likely to have a interconnected orientation to life and to be driven by a **Social Motivator.** Those with a Social Motivator focus on giving and on others and may even get angry with others who seem to have too much focus on the dollar and too little on the people involved.

People with a **Social Motivator** may possess the following talents and/or skills:

- *Empathy*

- *Altruism*

- *Helping others*

- *Identifying social issues*

- *Recruiting others to volunteer*

- *Championing a social cause*

- *Raising funds for charities*

TRADITIONAL

If you feel most comfortable working within a strong and efficient system, you may enjoy many of the following:

- *Supporting causes that affirm your beliefs*

- *Religion and religious piety*

- *Approaching change slowly*

- *Following systems for living*

- *Maintaining traditions*

You are most likely to have a strict and more conventional approach to life and be driven by a **Traditional Motivator.** Those with a Traditional Motivator will tend to believe they have found a system for living that works and, moreover, is correct.

People with a **Traditional Motivator** may possess the following talents and/or skills:

- *Strong commitment to right and wrong*

- *Strength of character*

- *Ability to analyze and execute systems consistently*

- *Seek higher meaning in life, nature, art, people, music and all other aspects of life*

- *Commit to causes*

- *Persuasion skills*

- *Boldness*

INDIVIDUALISTIC

The **Individualistic Motivator** is the most flexible of all six motivators. If you are drawn to achievement and enjoy many of the following:

- *Leading groups*

- *Being in the spotlight*

- *Overcoming challenges*

- *Thinking strategically*

- *Analyzing the big picture*

You are likely to have a strong desire for power and position and be driven by an **Individualistic Motivator.** People with an Individualistic Motivator find fulfillment in one or two of the other five motivators.

People with a strong **Individualistic Motivator** may possess the following talents and/or skills:

- *Be a visionary, adhering to beliefs that will advance a cause*

- *Have an ability to see the "big picture" and how the puzzle interlocks*

- *Form strategic relationships and key alliances*

- *Be willing to use power to accomplish purpose*

- *Gather and unify resources to accomplish purpose*

- *Seeking out highly competent individuals to surround them*

- *Comfort in a fast-paced environment*

As you read through each of these motivators as well as the talents and skills associated with each, you probably identified with one or more of the different types.

1. Which (Theoretical, Utilitarian, Aesthetic, Social, Traditional, Individualistic) stood out most to you?

2. Look at the list of skills and talents. From which group did you have the most?

3. What attitude do you possess?

Now, consider close friends, partners or business associates. **Can you detect the skills and talents listed among these six motivators in them? How well do you think you can blend your own attitude, given what you've learned about theirs?** These reflections can provide a powerful tool in honing your particular talents—and making the most of them.

THEORETICAL

UTILITARIAN

AESTHETIC

SOCIAL

TRADITIONAL

INDIVIDUALISTIC

PERSONAL SKILLS

From 60 WPM to Highly Motivated Self-Starters

Things have changed.

Years ago when skills were discussed during hiring, people generally were referring to hard skills, exact teachable abilities. Job advertisements specifically identified the minimum acceptable level of a skill, such as being able to "type 60 words per minute," or use shorthand. Things have changed. Today, we might see an online job posting stating the employer is seeking a "self-starter" who is "highly motivated." Soft skills are on the rise, as white-collar jobs grow to comprise a larger part of the job market. According to 2010 US Census data, **white collar workers make up 35 percent of the current occupations**, up from 15.9 percent in 1978, according to statistics from the U.S. Bureau of Labor Statistics.

We prefer to refer to these soft skills or competencies as personal skills. Personal skills are an important part of the selection and promotion process. Remember in Chapter 1, when Brenda was being considered for a job promotion? Her boss asked her what skills she had developed during her time with the company. Brenda's preparation fizzled when she heard the question. Personal skills develop slowly over time and are age-related but difficult to immediately identify. **For instance, you cannot read a book on teamwork and expect to transform into a team player.**

Skills are **an evolution** *of experiences.*

Teamwork is developed by working with people. If you are able to develop enough teamwork, you may develop your leadership skills. With leadership skills, your goal achievement skills will grow, as will your big picture view. With strong leadership and execution skills as well as a comprehensive entrepreneurial view, you may someday find yourself at the head of a company. Skills are an evolution of experiences.

Our research shows the more developed personal skills of college freshmen are teamwork and interpersonal skills. Consider those without very much experience. They still possess some personal skills, but not many. College freshmen have only begun to develop a few personal skills. Our research shows the more developed personal skills of college freshmen are teamwork and interpersonal skills. Decision-making is one of their weakest, as they have had little experience making decisions on their own. It is no surprise, then, that given the lack of decision-making skills they possess, college freshmen struggle with choices over field of study, class selection, amount of drinking and spending decisions. In a way, this is the worst possible point at which to send a person into an independent world where nearly every choice they make rests on their shoulders.

Imagine a stay-at-home mother who ten years ago left her job as an account executive at a technology company. While she used to have mastery over a specific set of job-related skills, she now believes her skill set is empty. But just as any office job builds skills, so too does non-office related skills.

The vast majority of stay-at-home mothers with ten years of experience possess the following personal skill set:

- *Time management*

- *Flexibility*

- *Goal setting*

- *Persuasion*

- *Self-management*

- *Budgeting*

- *Decision making*

- *Accountability*

- *Scheduling*

- *Leadership*

Weaving these personal skills into a re-sumé for returning to the workplace would help the stay-at-home mom and potential employers translate into familiar language the amount of mastery they have achieved.

Oddly enough, **recent research** we have conducted into our ability to determine our own strengths **has shown people are much better at determining what they are not skilled at than what they are very good at.** Using this premise, let's determine some personal skills you possess and which you may need to focus on improving.

Think of one of your greatest failures in business. **What went wrong? What didn't you do? What were you unable to complete? What part of the project carried the rest of the work down?** Next, consider job reviews you've had in the past. In your career history, what are the things you have been criticized for? How do those critiques translate into skills that were missing?

Make a list of these skills. Here is a general list of skills to help you consider your personal skills repertoire.

CONCEPTUAL THINKING

Conflict Management

CONTINUOUS LEARNING

creativity

Customer Focus

DECISION MAKING

Diplomacy & Tact

empathy

EMPLOYEE DEVELOPMENT/COACHING

Flexibility

FUTURISTIC THINKING

Goal Achievement

INTERPERSONAL SKILLS

Leadership

NEGOTIATION

Personal Accountability

Persuasion/Influencing Others

PLANNING & ORGANIZING

Presenting

Problem Solving Ability

RESILIENCY

Self Management

TEAMWORK

Understanding & Evaluating Others

written communication

Keep in mind that every business, every organization will have a unique set of skills they seek. They may even be called by a different name. The list we present to you is based off specific jobs and our experience with job benchmarking and nearly 30 years of research.

See the Resources Section on pg. 106 for a complete list of job skills definitions.

Mastering **all** *skills is not the key to success. It's about* **mastering the skills you need** *to achieve your personal goals.*

While this is a significant number of personal skills, keep in mind that mastering all skills is not the key to success. It's about mastering the skills you need to achieve your personal goals, to meet the requirements of the job and to achieve the goals of your company. Instead of looking to acquire random personal skills, consider your objectives and then amass the directly correlated skills to help you meet that goal. We'll discuss this in greater detail in the final chapter.

SKILLS ARE AN
EVOLUTION
OF EXPERIENCES

6

ACUMEN
Finding Order in
Your World

Have you ever had the opportunity to step back and watch children play and create? Inevitably, one will find his way into a leadership role, one will be corralling people, one will be focusing on the task associated with the playtime and one will be more cautious about the rules and boundaries. Essentially each child will develop his or her own filter as to how he or she sees the world. This worldview will impact the way in which they make decisions, judgments or place values on things.

We each have a lens through which we judge the world *and* ourselves.

The same is true of adults. We each have a lens through which we judge the world and ourselves. Our lens is filtered by what we see clearest. Think of yourself participating in an eye exam. As the doctor changes your lens, he asks, "Clearer? Foggier? Clearer? Foggier?" You will have a distinct lens through which you see best. Your business acumen is your individual judgment system through which you prioritize people, tasks or systems as they relate to the world. This judgment also applies to how you perceive who you are, what your roles are and where you want to be in the future.

Identifying your "clearest lens" is harder to do without an assessment. But if you are able to harness the information in order to position yourself for success, it will be a powerful transformation. Before diving into how to identify your lens, let's take a look at what each lens brings to the workplace and your personal ability to make decisions and problem solve.

Let's start with the three dimensions that discover how you view the world around you.

UNDERSTANDING OTHERS

The Understanding Others lens is about people. More precisely, it is how clearly you understand people. This dimension is often referred to as the "Feeling" dimension. A person with a strong ability to understand others and see this dimension clearly will have the following talents:

- *An understanding of people, friends and acquaintances*

- *Ability to be sensitive to and empathize with the life situations of others*

- *Clearly understanding people*

- *Interpersonal relationships*

- *Ability to see things from a people perspective*

- *Ability to appreciate others*

- *Ability to apply understanding of people*

- *Perception of the needs of others*

- *Ability to adapt to different people and behaviors*

PRACTICAL THINKING

The Practical Thinking lens is about tasks and resources and indicates how well one can focus on the tasks at hand and see all available resources. This is also referred to as the "Doing" dimension. A person with a strong ability to understand tasks and who sees this dimension clearly will have the following talents:

- *Practical comparison of tangible things, observable tasks and surrounding events and processes*

- *Ability to understand the functions of people at work*

- *Project management and attention to detail*

- *Understanding of work and labor processes*

- *Ability to adapt to different situations as they relate to tasks or things*

- *Understanding of all resources*

- *Ability to utilize all available resources*

SYSTEMS JUDGMENT

The Systems Judgment lens is about systems and processes. This will indicate how well one identifies with the systems and structures in the world and specifically the organization. This can also be looked at as the "Thinking" dimension. A person with a strong ability to understand systems and structure and sees this dimension clearly will have the following talents:

- *Comprehension of the ordering mechanisms of understanding*

- *Authoritative order: laws, policies, rules and procedures*

- *Thinking and planning as it relates to all concepts and ideas*

- *Ability to understand structure and order as it applies to the outside world*

- *Ability to understand the big picture and/or corporate objectives*

- *Understanding of policies, plans or superior changes*

Now that we understand the way in which people view the world, let's take a look at how we view ourselves.

SENSE OF SELF

The Sense of Self lens refers to the value in which you place on yourself as a person. What is your self-worth? This is also looking at who you are as a human being. Put another way we might think of this as "Who Am I?" A person with a clear understanding of his or her own self-worth will have the following talents:

- *Sense of inner worth*

- *A solid sense and understanding of one's reality*

- *The ability to give yourself credit and respect for the person you are*

- *Understands self identity, comfort in your own "skin"*

- *Knowledge of who you are and/or your own uniqueness*

- *Clarity of personal strengths, weaknesses, accomplishments and potential*

ROLE AWARENESS

The lens of Role Awareness indicates the identification one has with his or her life roles. This is not just professional, but applies to all life roles. This also can be referred to as "What I Am." A person with a clear understanding of his or her life roles will have the following talents:

- *Harmony and balance between personal and professional roles*

- *Clarity of various role duties and responsibilities*

- *Personal and/or professional role fulfillment*

- *Self-identification of roles in social situations*

- *Understanding one's place in the world*

SELF-DIRECTION

The Self Direction lens refers to how clearly you can see your future. Can you describe where you will be in great detail? This can also be referred to as "Who and What I Ought to Become." A person with a clear understanding of what his or her future will look like will have the following talents:

- *Self organization and discipline*

- *Clear self image and understanding of who I want to become*

- *Seeing unity within your future self*

- *Understanding the ideal self*

- *Understanding of self conduct and duty*

- *Ability to develop a path to reach the ideal self*

- *Understanding of the present and its application to the envisioned future*

- *Ability to bring one's envisioned future into the present*

As you can see from the information described, assessing one's acumen can be quite challenging. But it's not impossible.

IDENTIFYING ACUMEN

Let's start with how you view the world. Review each of the dimensions one more time. Then, pause for a moment to imagine yourself in a situation where you must solve a problem. **As most problems do, this problem contains the following elements for you to navigate: people, tasks and systems.** Note how you handle each element as you go through this process.

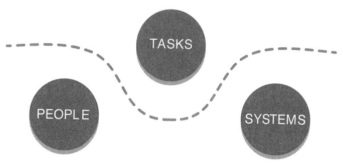

Once you've completed this reflection, consider: What was your primary focus as you handled this problem? What did you spend the most time and energy on? What other elements did you assume would fall into place if you handled your primary focus? If you had a people focus, most likely you possess the Understanding

Others lens. If you had a task focus, you probably have a Practical Thinking lens. If you had a system focus, it's likely you have a Systems Judgment lens.

Now review the following questions below to determine which appeal to your problem-solving process.

- *How will the solution impact people, or how can people help solve the problem?*

- *What resources can you utilize and how can you delegate or redistribute workload in order to get the problem solved?*

- *How does the solution fit within the existing system or what processes will need to be implemented in order to secure a successful outcome?*

As you select the questions above that resonate with you, which is the strongest, second strongest and finally the third? Each set of questions refers to a dimension, people or feeling, tasks or doing and then systems or thinking, in that order. The order of impact is an indicator of the order in which you place the "lenses" when making judgments about the world, specifically when making decision and solving problems. For example, if you placed the first question highest, you most likely place people first.

Understanding the order in which you evaluate problems and decisions will help you communicate your strengths. Go back to the skills associated with each of the dimensions and place an intensity rating to them that coincides with your lens order to better understand what skills you possess. It will be beneficial in articulating this information to a current or future employer, business partner or investor.

IDENTIFYING TALENTS

Now that you can articulate your talents as they relate to the outside world, let's move into your personal talents and how you view yourself. **For this side of acumen, we have simple questions for you to answer about yourself, which will indicate the order of your self-view lenses.**

- *How do you know when you are great? Is it a feeling you get or is it by an accomplishment or outside influence?*

- *What are you life roles? How long does it take for you to articulate all of your life roles?*

• *What does your future look like? In six months, two years, five years, and ten years?*

Which question was easiest to answer? The second easiest to answer? And finally the third? Each set of questions connects with a self-view lens. Who you are, what you are and who and what you ought to become. Again, understanding the order of your clarity for each of these dimensions and applying that to the attributes mentioned previously will be key in articulating your personal talents. The articulation of these attributes can be very difficult for people; if you can master this by applying the process outlined, you will stand out in business situations.

Once you are able to harness these as a part of your hidden talents, you will be able to maximize your performance and position yourself above the rest.

Remember, your acumen is deep inside you and can be difficult to pull to the surface. But once you are able to harness these as a part of your hidden talents, you will be able to maximize your performance and position yourself above the rest with confidence and poise.

OUR LENS IS
FILTERED
BY WHAT WE
SEE CLEAREST

7

EMOTIONAL INTELLIGENCE, EQ

Handling Life's Curveballs

Today's workforce is filled with buzzwords and jargon on topics of all types. Emotional Intelligence, or EQ as it is often referred, is no stranger to the buzz. Unlike many of the buzzwords that rise and fade quickly, research and performance studies are indicating there's a lot more substance to the soft science of EQ than skeptics first realized. While research is mounting, many are still unsure of exactly what EQ is and how they can identify it within themselves, let alone apply it to their personal and professional lives. Before we jump into the application of EQ, let's take a look at its foundation and what it really means.

EQ is all about change and your reaction to and anticipation of *that change.*

At its simplest form, EQ is all about change and your reaction to and anticipation of that change. We know the one consistent aspect of our world today is that it is constantly changing. Anytime change occurs, no matter how big or small, your EQ is working. If the change is of a positive nature or if the change is of a negative nature, your EQ still has to engage.

For the purpose of explanation, we are going to focus on negative changes that occur throughout your day. Let's say you are running late to work, dashing to get in your car when you realize your tire is flat. After changing the flat and starting off to work, you nearly collide with a car suddenly swerving into your lane on the highway. Essentially, three negative things have happened before your foot has even crossed the threshold of your workplace.

This type of negative activity coupled with a low EQ could technically destroy a person's productivity for the day. However, with a high EQ and the same amount of negative activity, a person may be able to redirect him or herself within an hour or two. While a high EQ lessens the impact, it still puts quite a significant dent in an individual's productivity, which is why building a high EQ is becoming one of the most important components in talent management today. **Professionals with a high EQ are more able to overcome challenges to their efficiency and remain engaged and on task, thus resulting in greater productivity for the organization.**

Having a high EQ doesn't mean you don't get angry or excited or emotional about things. It simply means you are able to re-center yourself faster than a person with a lower EQ. The TTI EQ model has five dimensions, each of which builds upon the others. **The five dimensions are as follows:**

- *SELF-AWARENESS*

- *SELF-REGULATION*

- *MOTIVATION*

- *EMPATHY*

- *SOCIAL SKILLS*

Let's review each of the dimensions as defined by Daniel Goleman and how they impact performance.

SELF-AWARENESS

Self-Awareness is the ability to recognize and understand your moods, emotions and drives, as well as their effect on others. **For example:**

- *Knowing how you're feeling and why*

- *Knowing your personal strengths and limits*

- *Having a sense of your self-worth and capabilities*

SELF-REGULATION

Self-Regulation is the ability to control or redirect disruptive impulses and moods and the propensity to suspend judgment and think before acting. **For example, a person with good self-regulation will display the following:**

- *Keeping disruptive emotions and impulses in check*

- *Maintaining standards of honesty and integrity*

- *Taking responsibility for personal performance*

- *Flexibility and handling change*

- *Being comfortable with novel ideas, approaches and new information*

MOTIVATION

Motivation is a passion to work for reasons that go beyond money or status and a propensity to pursue goals with energy and persistence. **It is exemplified by the following:**

- *Striving to improve or meet a standard of excellence*

- *Aligning with the goals of a group or organization*

- *Readiness to act on opportunities*

- *Persistence in pursuing goals despite obstacles and setbacks*

EMPATHY

Empathy is the ability to understand the emotional makeup of other people. **Those with high empathy are skilled at the following:**

- *Sensing others' feelings and perspectives and taking an active interest in their concerns*

- *Sensing others' development needs and bolstering their abilities*

- *Anticipation, recognizing and meeting the needs of others*

- *Cultivating opportunities through different kinds of people*

- *Reading a group's emotional currents and power relationships*

SOCIAL SKILLS

Social Skills are a proficiency in managing relationships and building networks. **Those with Social Skills are particularly suited for the following:**

- *Wielding effective tactics for persuasion*

- *Listening openly and sending convincing messages*

- *Negotiating and dissolving disagreements*

- *Inspiring and guiding individuals and groups*

- *Initiating or managing change*

- *Nurturing instrumental relationships for building bonds*

- *Working with others toward shared goals*

- *Creating group synergy in pursuing collective goals*

Our emotions have a physiological effect on us before we even realize it. This dates back to our human survival instincts of fight or flight. This natural instinct does not necessarily serve us well when it comes to making decisions in our personal and professional lives. **But by reviewing each of the above aspects of your EQ, you can determine what comes most naturally and what area needs more development.** You may be strong in one area and lacking in another. Review each aspect with this in mind. Pay particular attention to the Self-Awareness and Self-Regulation categories, as these will provide a base for further development.

Once you've assessed how these elements of EQ are present within you, you've begun to uncover your EQ. Who you are. What you do. How you react. And how you articulate the value you bring to situations.

Below you will see a series of pictures. **Take several moments to focus on each picture. Then, review the questions on the next page.**

Did you feel your body changing as you viewed the pictures? What emotions did you have as you viewed each picture? Did the emotions linger? How are you feeling now?

Everything you just described was your EQ at work. The trick is to utilize the dimensions. **Consider the following:**

- *Are you aware of your feelings?*

- *Are you able to manage your reactions?*

- *What is your motivation?*

- *Do you understand the potential impact your emotions have on others?*

- *Can you communicate in a way that will not negatively impact another's emotional state?*

Taking this basic understanding of EQ and applying it to everyday life is quite simple. A good way to begin this journey is to once again spend time focusing on Self-Awareness and Self-Regulation. For Self-Awareness, be sure to take your "Emotional Temperature" throughout the day. This will assist in your ability to assess your emotions. Self-Regulation can be a bit trickier because you need emotional enablers to re-center yourself. Emotional enablers can be things like pictures of loved ones, a voice mail from a happy customer or a happy moment that's easy to recall. Positive emotional interactions will help to regain a centered focus. Once you identify positive emotional enablers, be sure to have a few at hand for easy redirection. Focusing on these two elements alone will be a great aid toward building your EQ and understanding the EQ you possess.

Understanding and applying EQ in an organization allows people to **be** emotional without **getting** emotional. Mastering your ability to be aware of your emotions and then being able to manage their impact will instantaneously improve your decision-making and performance. **Others around you will respect you when you articulate your emotional temperature, instead of passively foisting a bad mood upon them.** Peers', colleagues' and employees' admiration for you will grow as you postpone important decision making from emotionally charged moments and instead make sound decisions after becoming re-centered. Harnessing and articulating your EQ will likely make you more sought after, as well.

CONCLUSION
Goal Setting Based on Your Talents

SETTING GOALS

As we discussed in the chapter on skills, mastering all skills is not the key to success. **Rather, mastering the key skills required to achieve your personal and career goals is the objective.** Instead of acquiring random skills consider your objectives and then amass the directly correlated skills to help you meet that goal. This begs the question, what are your goals, both in regards to your career and your personal life? Goals can change along the way, but in order to feel satisfied in your life, we recommend taking time to set clear, measurable goals for each, which will provide you with vital direction and inform the way you practice and implement the skills and talents you have now uncovered.

*Knowing what you are missing provides a map to **develop** those essential skills.*

Goal planning strategies are easy to come by. Many start with setting a goal and then proceed to lay out the steps to achieve that goal. Few, if any, pause between those steps to consider if the individual setting the goals possesses the behaviors, motivators, acumen, skills and EQ to actually take that step. If your goal is skydiving, the checklist that lays out the steps to your first skydive—signing up for a class, taking a training course, and jumping out of a plane—will be completely moot if you are afraid of heights. Without addressing your ability, or lack thereof, you'll never be able to achieve your goal. **Do you have the skills necessary to achieve your goals?** If not, that's OK, you can build them. Knowing what you are missing provides a map to develop those essential skills.

Let's assume your goal is to retire at 50. What skills, behaviors and motivators are necessary to achieve that goal? Certainly financial skills will be essential, both to plan for what you need to earn prior to your retirement and how to manage your money once you stop working. Let's assume you possess that skill. Part of your financial plan to achieve this goal is to invest and manage several real estate properties. Unfortunately, you don't have the time or the ability to manage real estate, so you begin paying a firm to do that for you, money which is now being diverted from your ultimate goal. In this example, the skills are there, but time constraints may inhibit part of your goal achievement. Just having a goal plan does not mean you are going to execute on the plan.

Bring to mind one of your goals, personal and professional. **Consider what you've uncovered about your known talents in the preceding chapters and reflect on the following:**

1. Identify the driving forces from behavior that will assist in achieving this goal.

2. Identify the motivators that will energize you to obtain the goal.

3. Identify the personal skills you currently have that will give you the ability to do this. Are there new personal skills you need to develop to complete the goal?

4. Remind yourself of your acumen. What is the priority order of your lens (people, task, system)? How does your acumen order affect your decision-making and get you closer to your goal?

5. Imagine typical obstacles to your goal. Imagine the feelings of frustration and discouragement. Now, prepare emotionally for overcoming those feelings. What can you do to minimize the impact of these natural reactions? Use your EQ to overcome these hurdles.

6. What prior experiences have you had that will help you achieve this goal? Are there new experiences you need to have to help you achieve this goal?

7. What knowledge do you possess that will assist you in achieving this goal? What new knowledge do you need to achieve this goal?

We consider this take on goal setting to be a more personal, individual and more effective approach. It takes into account the whole person, focusing on the hidden dimensions of talent explored throughout this book. **Using this strategy may help make goal achievement less like a wander and more like a clearly marked road map.**

CREATE A PATH TO YOUR GOAL

Your goal:

What motivates you to achieve this goal?

What skills do you have to help you achieve this goal?

What skills do you still need to amass to reach this goal?

How will you overcome challenges to this goal?

To amp up the efficacy even more, we recommend adding two more dimensions. Professional, validated and reliable assessments will augment your understanding of yourself in each of these areas. Using an assessment will solidify your hunches about your abilities, skills, motivators, EQ and acumen. (Of course, we recommend TTI's suite of assessments for this purpose.) In addition, we recommend selecting, hiring or partnering with an individual who can witness this goal-setting process and hold you accountable for what you are able to achieve.

Whether or not you pursue goal setting with a personal or professional coach or explore TTI's assessments, our goal here was to open your minds to the talents that often lay dormant and unidentified in most people. **Simply reflecting upon and knowing one's own talent can help you not only achieve more at work and home, it can help improve the quality of life and enhance overall happiness.**

We hope this book has helped you discover your talents with these seven different views in mind. We also hope employees and management are now better able to identify previously unknown talents and make the most of them, as this can lead to superior performance for the individual and for organizations. Since one's talents change due to life's experience and opportunities, we recommend revisiting "Talent: Unknown" regularly and continuing to uncover your own hidden talent.

RESOURCES

JOB SKILLS DEFINITIONS

Conceptual Thinking – The ability to analyze hypothetical situations or abstract concepts to compile insight.

Conflict Management – Addressing and resolving conflict constructively.

Continuous Learning – Taking initiative in learning and implementing new concepts, technologies and/or methods.

Creativity – Adapting traditional or devising new approaches, concepts, methods, models, designs, processes, technologies and/or systems.

Customer Focus – A commitment to customer satisfaction.

Decision Making – Utilizing effective processes to make decisions.

Diplomacy and Tact – The ability to treat others fairly, regardless of personal biases or beliefs.

Empathy – Identifying with and caring about others.

Employee Development/Coaching – Facilitating and supporting the professional growth of others.

Flexibility – Agility in adapting to change.

Futuristic Thinking – Imagining, envisioning, projecting and/or predicting what has not yet been realized.

Goal Achievement – The ability to identify and prioritize activities that lead to a goal.

Interpersonal Skills – Effectively communicating, building rapport and relating well to all kinds of people.

Leadership – Achieving extraordinary business results through people.

Negotiation – Facilitating agreements between two more parties.

Personal Accountability – A measure of the capacity to be answerable for personal actions.

Persuasion/Influencing Others – Convincing others to change the way they think, believe or behave.

Planning & Organizing – Utilizing logical, systematic and orderly procedures to meet objectives.

Presenting – Communicating effectively to groups.

Problem Solving Ability – Anticipating, analyzing, diagnosing, and resolving problems.

Resiliency – The ability to quickly recover from adversity.

Self Management – Demonstrating self control and an ability to manage time and priorities.

Teamwork – Working effectively and productively with others.

Understanding and Evaluating Others – The capacity to perceive and understand the feelings and attitudes of others.

Written Communication – Writing clearly, succinctly and understandably.

ABOUT THE
AUTHORS

BILL J. BONNSTETTER

Considered one of the pioneers in the assessment industry, Bill Bonnstetter has made significant contributions to the research and study of human behavior.

Bill was first to computerize both the DISC (Behaviors) and a Motivators assessment via his patented Internet Delivery Service (IDS®) and also holds the patents to TTI's job benchmarking process and employee success prediction system. A 2012 Edison Award nominee, Bill has been recognized for his innovation and excellence in the development, marketing and launch of new products and service.

His generosity and commitment to community has resulted in the gift of over a million dollars each year in free assessments for non-profit organizations, in addition to the time and resources donated through programs and partnerships such as The KEEN Project, TTI Family First and The Bonn Center. Bill is also the author of "If I Knew Then," and "The Universal Language DISC," which has sold more than 30,000 copies and is now in its fifteenth printing, as well as articles for the *Harvard Business Review*.

Contact him @bbonnstetter.

ASHLEY BOWERS

Ashley Bowers helps businesses and organizations effectively meet their human resource needs through research-based assessment solutions.

Ashley's leadership skills, business acumen and legal expertise have led the way to adverse impact and validity studies to meet the demands of the EEOC and OFCCP. Her participation on multiple business boards, and her collaboration with industry executives have contributed greatly to the development of new talent management solutions for hundreds of thousands of employees around the world.

Contact her @AshleyIBowers.